Earthrise:

Conscious Creation

of

UBUNTU/Contributionism

Communities

By

Michael Moriarty

©2017 by Michael Moriarty

All rights reserved.

ISBN 978-1-387-23778-4

Email: moriartym248@gmail.com

Contents

1. You Are Running Out of Time—Page 5
2. Some Wish to Cooperate, Some Wish to Separate: Splitting of the Two Earths—Page 9
3. Conscious Creation/Attraction of UBUNTU/Contributionism Communities—Page 13
4. Spiraling into Paradise on Earth: Getting Better at Your Passion—Page 17
5. Stewardship *versus* Ownership—Page 21
6. Facilitation, Synchronicity, and the Law of Attraction—Page 23
7. Unity Within Diversity—Page 27
8. Appropriate Technology—Page 29
9. Peace: Love is the Answer—Page 31
10. Earth is Your Home—Page 33
11. Family and Relationships—Page 37
12. Education—Page 39
13. The Time is Now: the New Humans—Page 43

Chapter One

You Are Running Out of Time

In this chapter, I discuss the reasons why it is urgent that those who wish to create/attract the experience of living in an UBUNTU/Contributionism Community begin to do so soon.

At the time of this writing, there is no viable alternative to the current economic and political order *other than* UBUNTU/Contributionism. The only known economic and political system that meets the requirement of individual Humans to follow their passions (their joy: what makes them happy) is UBUNTU/Contributionism. The only known economic and political system that meets the requirements of Humanity, as a collective, to care for one another and for the Earth is UBUNTU/Contributionism. Furthermore, UBUNTU/Contributionism is the only known economic and political system that enables Humanity to meet the three requirements of Open Contact: being more loving to one another; to our Agarthan brothers and sisters; and to the Earth.

In short, the economic and political foundation of a 4th Density Earth *will be* UBUNTU/Contributionism Communities (UCs).

Before I go any further, I should note that it will be assumed, in what follows, that the reader is familiar with the concepts discussed in my first book, *The Awakening of Humanity: What You Need to Know.* Although I shall repeat, here, some of what was written there, for the most part, I will seek to avoid such repetition. If you are unfamiliar with some of the concepts discussed in this book, you will find them explained in my first book. I ask that you read that work before reading this one.

The current economic and political order will, likely, collapse by 2024. By 2027, it is a virtual certainty that it will have done so. Thus, UCs should be in existence and operation *before* those dates, and—if you wish to avoid catastrophe, yourself—*you should be living in one.*

All change is instantaneous. If it appears to you that certain changes take time—perhaps a lot of time—to manifest, the amount of time elapsed merely reflects your belief that you need that amount of time in order to reach the decision that you will change. Once you decide to change, the change is instantaneous. Thus, in theory, you could manifest the experience of living in a UC instantaneously and, hence, there is no need to *begin a process* of manifestation—much less, to begin *now.*

In practice, very few people, currently, believe that they *can* instantly manifest their thoughts, consistently, in the waking state. This very belief—that they cannot do so—manifests as an inability to do so. Indeed, the great majority of Humans don't believe that they can manifest their thoughts *at all* in the waking state, much less instantaneously. Of those who *do* believe that they can manifest their thoughts/what they focus their attention upon in the waking state, the vast majority believe that a process is required, and that that process takes time (perhaps, a lot of time).

So, if you wish to experience living in a UC before 2024 or 2027, the sooner you start, the more likely you will succeed. Because of your belief that manifestation requires a process and, hence, takes time, you could wait until it's *too late* to begin your manifestation process.

It is evident from the fact that, currently, there are no UCs in existence that very few are focusing their attention upon/thinking about living in a UC (at least, not enough for that thought/focus to become their dominant vibration, or point of attraction). Hence, it is safe to conclude that *all those who wish to live in a UC by 2024 or 2027 should begin to focus their attention upon/think about doing so now. You must think about/focus your attention upon this until it becomes the dominant vibration within you.*

Chapter Two

Some Wish to Cooperate, Some Wish to Separate:
Splitting of the Two Earths

In this chapter, I explain the relationship between the Law of Attraction and the energetic separation of the 3rd- and 4th-Density Earths. The point is made in order to underscore the notion that a UC cannot be manifested by someone subscribing to a 3rd Density belief in separation.

The Law of Attraction (LOA) states that *that which is like unto itself, is drawn.* If your dominant vibration is x, then the LOA can bring to you thoughts, people, circumstances, objects, events, etc., that are similar to x, but it cannot bring to you thoughts, people, circumstances, objects, events, etc., that are highly-dissimilar to x. This idea is the basis for the energetic separation of the 4th- from the 3rd-Density Earth.

You are the sole creator/attractor of your reality, your Earth. Your physical reality—your Earth—exists as a mirror, reflecting back to you your most-strongly held beliefs. In short, *you are the Earth that you think that you are on.* Likewise, you are the Density that you think that you are a part of.

Hence, the separation of Earth into a 3rd Density Earth and a 4th Density Earth is, in truth, a reflection of the separation of the Collective Consciousness of Humanity into two Collective Consciousnesses. One Collective Consciousness reflects a 3rd Density reality (Earth), while the other reflects a 4th Density reality (Earth), as the dominant vibration of the Collective Consciousness in the former case is significantly lower than that of the Collective Consciousness in the latter case.

One can see from the above that, as the dominant vibration of one mass of Humanity increases relative to the dominant vibration of the other, there will come a point where the LOA will not be able to bring to a person in the lower-frequency group thoughts, people, circumstances, events, objects, etc., that members of the higher-frequency group can access (via the LOA). Indeed, at some point, the two Earths will be *physically separated,* as the LOA will not be able to bridge the energetic divide. It will be as if an impenetrable barrier separated them into two distinct realities, two distinct Earths.

The Great Shift from a 3rd Density Earth to a 4th Density Earth (for those who are choosing to make the Shift) is upon us. To be sure, it will take approximately 50-100 years to reach completion (physical separation); nonetheless*, the Shift has begun.* Note, too: long before physical separation occurs, many thoughts, people, circumstances, events, objects, etc., will have become inaccessible to those of the lower-frequency group. They *do not have* 50-100 years to manifest a UC, even if the current economic and political system were not to collapse before then.

The belief in separation of man from man is, perhaps, the quintessential 3rd Density belief. It is a belief that underwrites the entire political and economic order of 3rd Density Human civilization. Remove that belief, and the entirety of the economic and political system would fall apart.

UCs, by contrast, are based upon a belief in the unity of Mankind. In such an economic and political system, there is no separation, competition, or rivalry (and there certainly are no enemies); there is only cooperation. This belief—the belief in the essential unity of all of Mankind—is a true 4th Density belief.

So, a person subscribing to a belief in separation must jettison that belief soon if they are not to find themselves experiencing an economic and political collapse, without the ability to manifest, for themselves, the experience of living in a UC. In all likelihood, many such persons will not be able to physically survive the collapse of the 3rd Density economic and political order.

Chapter Three

Conscious Creation/Attraction of UBUNTU/Contributionism Communities

In this chapter, I show that, by creating/attracting a UC through your thought or what you focus your attention upon, all the components necessary for the experience of living in a UC come together in an effortless manner. Furthermore, when you create/attract a UC (or anything, truly) through your thought—and not through your action—it is less likely that much (or any) struggle will be involved with those who do not desire to be a part of your creation.

You get what you think about or focus your attention upon, whether you want it or not. This is the fundamental basis of reality creation/attraction, and it applies to the creation/attraction of *any* kind of reality—whether it be an object, event, person, thought, circumstance, information, or a UC. This way of reality creation/attraction, through a correct use of the Universal Law of Attraction, places you at One with the power of the Universe, and allows you—via your Higher Self, which is directly-connected to the Creator of All That Is—to create/attract anything that you desire, effortlessly.

This is how you will create/attract your UC: by focusing your attention upon it so diligently, and by thinking about it so frequently, that it becomes *the dominant vibration* within you. This point is crucial: you will attract to you whatever reality represents the vibrational essence of your point of attraction, so you must make certain that you are focusing upon/thinking about, to a degree high-enough to evoke strong positive emotion within you, living in a UC. Remember, too, that every subject is, really, two subjects: what you want and what you don't want (or the absence, or lack, of what you want). To sort out whether you are predominantly focused upon/thinking about what you want (to live in a UC) rather than what you don't want (not living in a UC, or the absence of living in a UC, currently), pay attention to how you feel. If you feel good, then you are focused upon/thinking about what you want. Keep thinking such thoughts. If you feel bad, then you are focused upon/thinking about what you do *not* want. Reach for the best-feeling thought that you have access to in the moment, even if it feels only a *little* better than your current thought. If you keep doing this, you will be able, over time, to shift your thoughts to thoughts that feel *much* better than your current thought, and such thoughts will attract to you what you desire.

What would happen if you were to take action to create a UC *before* you had practiced the thought of living in a UC until it had become your dominant vibration? You would get the vibrational essence of whatever thoughts *were* dominant within you. In this case, *you would not obtain the reality you desire: the experience of living in a UC.* Furthermore, whatever results you managed to achieve in the direction of your desire would be meager; and it would require hard work even to achieve those (poor) results.

When you create through your actions, without regard to what your vibrational offering is, you are far more likely to encounter the opposition of those who do not wish to be a part of your creation (in this case, a UC), than you would encounter were you to create your desire through your thoughts/ through what you are focusing your attention upon. Remember: you get more of what you oppose; for, by opposing anything, you activate the vibration of it within yourself. By not paying attention to your vibrational offering, you are more likely to attempt to create by opposing that which you do not desire (in this case, the current economic and political order). Not only is this approach counter-productive, *it is not even necessary.*

Indeed, *by thinking about/focusing upon interacting only with those who are in harmony with your desire to live in a UC, you can avoid, entirely, encountering anyone who opposes your desire to live in a UC (and you will encounter only those who seek to aid you in achieving your desire).* Thus, only by creating/attracting your desired reality through your thoughts, will it manifest effortlessly and without struggle, strife, or force.

How do you know if the action you are thinking about will aid you in achieving the reality that you desire to experience? Simple: pay attention to how that thought feels. Does it feel good? If so, then that is communication from your Higher Self telling you that that action would, were you to perform it, help you to achieve your desire (in this case, living in a UC). On the other hand, if the thought feels bad, then this is a message from your Higher Self letting you know, in the moment, that the performance of the action in question would *not* aid you in achieving your desire (and may create/attract an experience that you do *not* desire).   In this way, through creating/attracting a UC by what you think about/focus upon, you will be led—by your Higher Self—to perform the perfect actions, in the perfect timing, to manifest the reality that you desire to experience.

If you pay attention to how you feel, and always reach for the best-feeling thought that you have access to in the moment, you will be unerringly guided, by your Higher Self, to the thoughts and actions that will create for/attract to you the life that you seek (living in a UC). By only, and always, reaching for and doing what feels good—in short, by following your joy, your passion—you will find that what you seek (life in a UC), is seeking you. And—bonus!—you will always feel good. What could be a better plan than that?

Chapter Four

Spiraling Into Paradise on Earth: Getting Better at Your Passion

In this chapter, I discuss why, in all likelihood, you will manifest a high-functioning UC through a *series* of manifestations—and not through a single manifestation event.

What you manifest through what you think about or focus your attention upon is dependent upon your understanding of what it is that you truly want. Most of you, currently, have *some* understanding of what a functioning UC would consist of, or look like. However, very few of you, currently, know what a *high-functioning* UC would look like. How could you? You don't know what you don't know.

Fortunately, however, it is not necessary to get where you desire to be in one, giant step. You can get there via a series of smaller steps. As you take a step, you learn from the experience. Using the knowledge gained, you are in a position to refine your understanding of what it is that you truly want. With that improved understanding, you will, then, create/attract an *improved version* of what you desire. You can continue this process as often as you wish, much like traveling up a spiral, rung after rung. It is the spiral of your *imagination.*

Let's make this idea more concrete. Think about/focus your attention upon living in a UC, as you currently conceive what that is (how *else* could you do it?). In practical terms, this means to *imagine yourself, with as much clarity and detail as you can, living a joyful life in a UC.* Imagine this often, many times a day—every day. The more that you imagine it, the happier you feel doing so. If you do this often enough, living in a UC will become your point of attraction and, as a consequence, you will be inspired to take certain actions—actions that will facilitate living in a UC. Likewise, the resources that you need to live in a UC will come to you. Similarly, people who want to live in a UC with you, or who want to help you to live in a UC, will come into your life. Circumstances that favor your living in a UC will line up for you. In the end, you will find yourself living in a UC. You might be amazed, looking back over the journey, as to how you got there—but you got there!

As you live your daily life in the UC that you created/attracted, you will observe things, and learn from those observations. Perhaps you'll notice that, although you love to garden (let's say that that is your passion and, thus, your contribution to your UC), you, currently, are not very good at it. *Of course* you aren't very good at it, yet: you need more experience at practicing your passion. After all, in the old economic and political system, you worked at a job doing something *other than* your passion, and that is one of the main reasons why you weren't happy within the old system. Other members of your UC are in a similar situation as you, and for the same reason.

You'll notice some things about your UC that work quite well, and other details that could be improved. Not a problem: you and the other members of your UC can, each, use the improved understanding of what it is that each of you truly wants from his/her experience of living in a UC (what that looks like), to create/attract, through your imaginations, an *improved version* of your/their current UC.

In the second iteration of your UC, you'll notice that, although there are still some issues to resolve, there are far fewer of them than before. Additionally, those things that were functioning quite well in the first iteration of your UC are, now, functioning *even better*.

You can continue this process of refinement of your UC as much as you like. You will never reach perfection; for perfection is an ideal, and ideals, by definition, cannot be achieved in the physical realm. Nonetheless, you can, through this process, create/attract a high-functioning UC. At some point in this process, you will look around your UC and feel that, truly, you have created/attracted Paradise on Earth.

As you continue this process of refinement of your UC, climbing the spiral rung by rung, you will gain more practice at your passion. As a consequence, your contribution to your UC will improve, and your fellow UC members will benefit from that improvement. Likewise, the other members of your UC will gain more experience at *their* passions, and you will benefit from their improvement. Shared benefits.

You, and they, are climbing the spiral *together.*

Chapter Five

Stewardship *versus* Ownership

In this chapter, I discuss how a shift to UCs will necessitate a radical change in viewpoint regarding money, property, and possessions. This change in viewpoint will have far-reaching implications.

During a transitional stage to a fully-functioning UC, the members of a given UC may choose to utilize a certain amount of money in their dealings with those outside of their UC. However, this is meant only as a temporary measure: a fully-functioning UC utilizes no money, no barter, and no trade.

In a fully-functioning UC, the concept of ownership—of money, real estate, housing, cars, inventions, furniture, books, pets, spouses, or of *anything*—is replaced with that of stewardship. The essence of ownership is control and separation, while the essence of stewardship is caretaking and unity.

Stewardship does *not* mean that you are responsible *for* others, *for* the Community, or *for* the Earth. It means that you are responsible *to* others, *to* the Community, and *to* the Earth. You are, however, 100% responsible *for* your choices: *you* will reap whatever *you* sow.

As an individual member of a UC, you will not own any property of any kind. Nor does the UC, as a collective, own anything. All resources, of whatever kind, utilized within the UC are understood to be available to all members of the UC, and every resource that you need to follow your passion will be made available to you. As, obviously, you cannot follow your passion if you are not alive, this means that you will be provided with food, water, clothing, housing, etc., as well as with items more-specific to your individual passion.

You are a steward, or caretaker, of your fellow Human Beings (whether they live in your UC, or not); of your UC, as a collective; and of the Earth (whether it is that portion of the Earth that your UC sits on, or any other). In this latter capacity, over time (as Open Contact unfolds), you will find it helpful to work, not only with your fellow UC members (and with other Humans from outside your UC), but also with the Agarthans, some extraterrestrial species (especially, with those Hybrid children born off-planet), and with *elementals and the plants and animals, themselves.*

As your consciousness shifts from 3rd- to 4th-Density, it is inevitably realized that many of the possessions that, in 3rd Density, you thought were necessary or helpful, are, in truth, a burden to you. It is somewhat ironic that, even as the abundance of the Universe becomes freely-available to you as a conscious creator/attractor of your life experience, you will have less desire for lots of material possessions. Many of you have already begun to notice this change in yourselves. It is a reflection of spiritual growth: you are traveling up the Spiral of Light, to planes of consciousness that are less-dense, less material.

As you become less-enamored of material possessions, your feelings of being the recipient of great abundance will grow. Not only can you manifest (through what you think about/focus your attention upon) anything that you wish; but, also, it takes far less material abundance to satisfy you. When you can get more from less, then you will be able to do less and get more. Life becomes easier, more harmonious, and richer.

Chapter Six

Facilitation, Synchronicity, and the Law of Attraction

In this chapter, I explain how the shared core beliefs of the members of a UC are used to guide decision-making in Community meetings. Also, I explain the role of Facilitators of Synchronicity in economic and political matters within the UC.

The members of a UC have synchronistically attracted one another, via the Law of Attraction, in order to form their UC. They have been brought together by their Higher Selves by, each, thinking about/focusing his/her attention upon what he/she wants to experience (any person who is attracted to the UC by thinking about/focusing his/her attention upon what he/she does *not* want will not remain long in the UC). Thus, we can conclude that, *by definition*, the members of the UC share common, core values (beliefs).

As the members of the UC share common, core values, *automatically they are unified and work together harmoniously.* Mind you, it is not that there are walls around the UC keeping those who do not share the same core values out. No. Rather, it is that those who do not share the same common, core values are not attracted to the UC in the first place.

Those who take 100% responsibility for their choices are *self-governing.* They do not need *anyone* to act as an authority over them. Thus, *no one within the UC has power over another.* Harmony, not chaos, ensues because each person can be relied upon to, while following his/her passion, synchronistically do what is best for himself/herself *and* for the group, as a result of his/her sharing the same core values as the other members of the group.

Thus, in a UC, there is no need for laws to dictate to the members of the UC what they can, and cannot, do. This obviates the need for any form of law-enforcement: police officers, lawyers, judges, juries, prisons, wardens, etc., are simply not necessary.

Let us discuss the role of the Facilitators of Synchronicity within the UC. Be it noted that these persons do not have any authority over anyone in the UC; they cannot tell anyone what they can, or cannot, do. What, then, *can* they do? They perform, within the UC, two principal functions. First, within the economy, they help to connect those who have goods or services to those who need them. Second, they help to guide (while taking no position, themselves) the discussions at Community meetings.

In this latter role, the Facilitator will identify the values inherent in any given proposal that arises as a result of discussion among the UC members at the Community meetings, and determine whether or not those values are aligned with the shared common, core values of the members of the UC. If so, the proposal can proceed. If not, it does not. Note that it does not matter how many people are for or against a given proposal. All that matters is that the proposal be in alignment with the common, core values of the UC. However, if a situation arises where all members of the UC wish to act on a proposal that is not in alignment with their common, core values, they can adjust their common, core values by consensus, and the proposal can, then, go forward.

In many instances, there may be more than one way of proceeding that is in accord with the common, core values of the UC. In that case, all ways will be tried. With experience, it may be discovered that one way is superior to the others; that more than one way will work; or that none of the ways tried works. All individual expressions that are consistent with the common, core values of the UC will be honored.

As the members of the UC gain experience at conscious creation/attraction of their life experiences (at paying attention to how they feel, and always reaching for the best-feeling thought that they have access to in the moment), they will find that, more and more, their Higher Selves are placing them in the right place at the right time to achieve everything that they desire to experience. Eventually, they will *always* be in the right place at the right time. On that day, the Facilitators of Synchronicity will no longer be needed, as synchronicity will no longer need facilitation.

Chapter Seven

Unity Within Diversity

In this chapter, I illustrate how the diversity inherent within the Human family is a blessing and a reflection of the Wisdom and Compassion of the Creator.

The members of a UC share the same common, core beliefs and are, thus, automatically unified. Yet, each individual member of the UC is completely unique. The Creator does not make mistakes; nor does It need "do-overs"—It gets everything right the first time, every time. Hence, there is *only one you.* There never has been, nor will there ever be, another Being like you. This is true of *every* Being in the Creation. Hence, each Being is *precious*, and is to be honored for his/her/its unique contribution to the Whole.

In point of fact, it is those very differences between us that make possible the joy of each of us. Within the UC, I am free to follow my passion, to do what brings me joy, because I know that all those other things that need to get taken care of—things that I am *not* passionate about—will get taken care of by other members of the UC who *are* passionate about just those things. And I perform the same service for them, enabling them to follow their own, individual passions.

Can you not see the Wisdom and Compassion of the Creator in this? You live in a benevolent Cosmos.

Reflecting further upon this, we realize that there really is *no way* to place a value on anyone's contribution to the Whole—other than to say that it is *priceless*. And, it doesn't matter *what* that contribution is: if it enables you to live your joy--to you, it is truly priceless.

Do you not see the great gift that your brother or sister is giving to you? Everyone's contribution is needed; everyone is needed.

Each member of the UC is, thus, supporting each and every other member of the UC: we are One.

Chapter Eight

Appropriate Technology

In this chapter, I discuss the application of technology in the context of a UC.

As the members of a UC share a belief in, and a commitment to, sustainable living, natural means to achieving our purposes will always be preferable to artificial means, all other things being equal. For the members of a UC, technology is an adjunct to, and not an essential focus of, life. It must always be used only in a way that is life-affirming and respectful of the dignity of all Beings. The highest technologies available may be used, as long as they are used in this way.

The history of Mankind has shown numerous examples of the power of technology outstripping the level of consciousness of people to utilize it in a responsible manner. The members of a UC should reject any technology that they cannot, at their current level of consciousness, utilize in a life-affirming way. They must find another way to achieve their ends, or reconsider their need to achieve those ends.

As the members of a UC share a belief in the sacredness of all Life, including Human life, they reject the so-called Transhumanism Agenda. Each member of a UC is here to do the internal work necessary to continue up the Spiral of Light back to the Godhead. If they do their work, they are capable of achieving *far more* than any technology will *ever* achieve. There are *no* shortcuts up the Spiral of Light, including technological shortcuts.

As one travels up the Spiral of Light to less-dense planes of existence, one naturally tends to become less interested in material things, including technology. Instead, one tends to become more interested in the exploration of consciousness, which is what one is. Technology, on the other hand, is merely a mirror of what you, as consciousness, are capable of achieving.

The members of a UC reject the use of cloning technology. Cloned Beings are *not* manifestations of Soul and, additionally, are Soulless. Because of this, they are *not* part of the Divine Plan: they are *life without meaning or purpose.*

Even if one had the permission of a Soul to transfer it to another physical body and, also, the technology to do so, this would *still* represent an attempt to step outside of the Divine Plan. The members of a UC, thus, reject the indefinite extension of physical life beyond that intended by the Soul prior to its incarnation.

Chapter Nine

Peace: Love is the Answer

In this chapter, I explain how it is that a UC does not require an army to protect itself.

The members of a UC are, each, conscious creators/attractors of their own life experiences. It is a shared belief of the members of such a Community that peaceful and harmonious relations with all Beings is the preferred reality.

You get what you think about/focus your attention upon, whether you want it or not. If you think fearful thoughts—e.g., that others seek to harm you—then you will attract experiences of others seeking to harm you. On the other hand, *if you think only loving thoughts*—e.g., thoughts of peaceful and harmonious relations with others—then you will attract *only* experiences of peaceful and harmonious relationships with others.

In this way, the members of a UC obviate the need for an army or other physical force to protect them from "enemies". If you think that you have enemies that you need to be protected from, then you will have: you will, through that very thought, invite them into your experience. Remember: absolutely *no* Being can assert itself into your experience without your invitation. What you think about/focus your attention upon *is* your invitation.

It is worth recalling, too, that you get more of anything that you oppose. As an example, if you think about how much you dislike war and violence; or, if you focus your attention upon war and violence (say, by reading newspaper accounts of war and violence); then you are activating the vibration of war and violence within yourself.

Consequently, the Law of Attraction will return to you the vibrational essence of what you are thinking about/focusing your attention upon: more experiences of war and violence for you to dislike.

Again, as always: loving thoughts are the answer. If you only think about/focus your attention upon having peaceful and loving relationships with others—whether those others are inside or outside of your UC—then those are the only realities that you will experience. It really is as simple as that.

A hatred of war will bring more war. Only a love of peace will bring peace.

Chapter Ten

Earth is Your Home

In this chapter, I discuss some of the implications of sustainable living, a core belief of UC members.

Sustainable living is a way of life, not merely a department within life. It involves living in such a way that the Earth can easily support us. It is based upon a fundamental understanding of our Oneness with the Earth; an understanding that we are a *part of* the Whole, and not *apart from* the Whole. It is an expression of our undying love for the Creator and the Creation.

Each UC will establish its own set of Community Projects (which may vary over time). One or more of these Projects might be dedicated to tasks specifically related to sustainable living concerns—e.g., an Environmental Rehabilitation and Wildlife Habitat Preservation Community Project. However, *sustainable living will inform all activities within all Community Projects, and all activities outside of the Community Projects.* As just one example of this, all food will be grown using organic methods.

As the old economic and political system collapses, the members of the UC, as caretakers of the Earth, will be directly involved in the work of cleaning-up the debris of the old civilization, and in removing the pollution from the soils, air, and waters of the Earth. The goal of this massive rehabilitation effort will be to restore as much of the Earth as possible to a completely natural, pristine condition.

Each UC is directly involved in caretaking the local environment of the UC. It may be helpful to work together with neighboring UCs in order to take care of the environment outside of the immediate vicinity of one's UC.

It is recognized that we, the Human Beings on the surface of the Earth, are co-caretakers of Gaia, along with our Inner Earth brothers and sisters. Thus, we seek to work hand-in-hand with the Agarthans in cleaning-up the Earth, and in maintaining the Earth as a Garden of Eden.

Likewise, we seek to work in harmony with our extraterrestrial friends and relatives in restoring the Earth to its natural, pristine condition. However, we acknowledge that this work is, principally, ours: *we* created the mess, *we* must clean it up.

We must open-up, via the use of our consciousnesses, the lines of communication with the elementals, plants, and animals. Currently, there are some Human Beings who can communicate with these Beings. It should be a goal of each member of a UC to acquire this ability. We need to learn from the elementals, plants, and animals, *themselves,* what it is that they desire. Also, they can tell us the best way of assisting them. (Bonus: look at how many new *friends* we will make....)

The assistance that these Beings offer *us*, day after day, is priceless. When we learn to communicate with them, and really begin to *listen* to what they have to tell us, a new day will dawn. We have *not even begun* to tap the wisdom of the Living Library. The assistance that they will be able to give to us, then, will make us feel truly blessed.

Our ancestors, whenever they picked a fruit from a tree, *asked permission* of the tree for the *gift* of the fruit. Doing so was an acknowledgement of the tree's status as a conscious, sovereign, living Being—and an acknowledgement, as well, of the tree's contribution to Human welfare. This ancient path, a path of *gratitude* for the gifts of Nature, is one that the members of a UC would do well to return to.

It does not matter how many lifetimes you have spent in other star systems; nor does it matter to what other star systems you may, eventually, take yourself. In this moment, you are a Human Being incarnate on Earth: *this* is your home. You belong here.

Chapter Eleven

Family and Relationships

In this chapter, I discuss some aspects of family and relationships that are prominent in a 4th Density energetic environment.

Fourth Density is a heart-centered environment. As the members of a UC are conscious creators/attractors of their life experiences, they are allowers. They understand that they are the sole creators/attractors of their own experiences. Further, they understand that what others intend, think, feel, say, or do cannot harm them if they choose not to invite those others into their experience by focusing upon them or by thinking about them (or by not focusing upon/thinking about that aspect of the others in question, they will not experience that aspect of them). Thus, the members of a UC are capable of expressing unconditional love for others: they can truly love *without condition*, as they allow others to be, do, or have anything that they wish to be, do, or have.

The members of a UC understand, too, that they cannot express unconditional love for anyone else if they do not, first, extend it to themselves: what is within will be reflected without. Loving himself/herself unreservedly allows each to know that he/she is worthy of creating/attracting for himself/herself a life of joy. What is within will be reflected without. Thus, to truly help others, you have to help yourself, first. You cannot escape yourself. This is not selfishness; it is wisdom.

Being able to love without condition—being an allower—implies, among other things, that possessiveness in relationships ceases to exist. This does not mean that people cannot have exclusivity in relationships, if that is their joy. However, many UC members would, likely, choose to adopt more open relationships with others. In either case, however, allowers—by definition—are not jealous.

Fourth Density, as the Density of Love, carries with it its own challenges. For example, some UC members may find it difficult, as unconditionally loving Beings, to maintain proper boundaries with others. A recognition that, in such cases, one is no longer allowing but, instead, attempting to control, should prove helpful.

When one achieves a state of allowing, the state of unconditional love, one's concept of family becomes larger; indeed, it grows to encompass the entirety of the Creation. Certainly, then, a member of a UC views each and every other member of the UC as family. This has profound implications for child rearing.

Yes, in 4th Density, children will continue to be created and come into the World in the usual way. However, they, and their parents, will have lots of support in 4th Density. The parents of a child will be able to trust that, no matter where in the UC their child roams, he/she will be loved and cared for. The child, in turn, will become familiar with many and, thus, come to appreciate, at an early age, the value in the diversity of the Human family. In addition, this will give the child opportunities to learn many things, safe to explore the World and learn what he/she is passionate about.

Chapter Twelve

Education

In this chapter, I discuss the process of education in a UC.

The truest indicator of success in life is happiness (joy). As, broadly speaking, it is the function of education to help people to be successful in life, this idea—that *happiness is the true measure of success*—must be the guiding star of all education within the UC.

None of the indigenous peoples of the World have ever had a formal educational system. The reason for this is simple: such a system is not needed and, even on its own merits, makes little sense. A UC does not have a formal educational system, either—for the same reasons. Life is our school.

As we saw in the previous chapter, the child will, naturally, interact with the adult members of the UC, learning, in the process, what he/she enjoys doing or learning about. The members of the UC will provide the child with every opportunity to learn more about what he/she expresses an interest in. The Facilitators of Synchronicity can help smooth the way, if that is necessary.

Each member of the UC is a conscious creator/attractor of his/her own life experience. Thus, each member of the UC understands that, if someone (child or adult) appears before them seeking to learn what they know, then they must have co-created that experience with the seeker. Hence, they are the teacher and the seeker is their apprentice. They will teach the apprentice what they know.

All knowledge and technology available to *any* member of the UC is available to *all* members of the UC. For example, there are no patents, copyrights, or trademarks in the UC. Any technology or process invented by anyone in the UC is made freely available to all other members of the UC. We share freely with one another.

It is understood that education, broadly conceived, is a lifelong endeavor. Thus, *all* will have opportunities to explore more of their interests/passions, to explore more of who they are. A person is not limited to one passion in life.

Currently, there are some Human Beings who can access at least *some* of the information within their DNA (the Akashic Record). Over time, as the members of a UC evolve in 4th Density, more and more of them will acquire this ability. Indeed, the amount and variety of information available from this source will increase. The development of this ability should be an objective of each member of the UC.

With the development of this ability, each member of the UC will *be able to acquire the specific knowledge and skills that they desire, when they desire it.*

Furthermore, as the members of the UC acquire the ability to communicate with the elementals, plants, and animals, a tremendous amount of knowledge will become available to them. Any member of the UC, child or adult, will then be able to access and make use of this knowledge, as well.

As Open Contact unfolds, knowledge, skills, and technology will be made available to the members of the UC by our Inner Earth and extraterrestrial friends and relatives. This information and technology will be freely available to all members of the Community, as is *all* information and technology.

Bear in mind that, as the members of a UC evolve in 4th Density, their telempathic abilities will increase. All Human Beings are, naturally, telempathic; however, currently, only *some* Humans are able to send/receive telempathic messages *consciously*. Not only will the increasing ability of UC members to consciously send/receive telempathic messages facilitate the teaching and learning process, but *it will, also, force the ending of all secrets and lies.*

Chapter Thirteen

The Time is Now: the New Human

From choosing to play the "game of limitation" within the construct of time, to choosing to live their unlimited potential within the Now moment, this is the journey of the New Humans, the Gods who have awakened.

You are God, the Creator of All That Is. *Everything* that you have ever experienced has been created/attracted to you, by you. *Everything* that you are now experiencing is being created/attracted to you, by you. *Everything* that you will ever experience will be created/attracted to you, by you. What you experience always has been; always is; and always will be *your choice.*

You are awakening to the truth of your Godhood. You freely-chose to give yourself the experience of limitation, of *forgetting* that you are the Creator. Only by *completely* forgetting your connection to Source, your Higher Self, could you truly have the experience of limitation. Only in this way could you appear to give away your sovereignty to others. Only in this way could you *believe* that you were *not* unconditionally loving and infinitely knowledgeable— capable and worthy of making your own decisions--but, instead, were a helpless victim of others. Since you *are* the Creator, and you create through what you believe, you perceived yourself as a helpless victim of others.

The past does not *cause* the present. Memories are created in the "now" moment. Both the past and the future are created in the present moment. You are completely free, in the present moment, to choose to create/attract *any* experience that you wish to have. There are no conditions on your power to create: you are *unlimited.*

What will you choose to create/attract?

If you choose to create/attract the experience of living on a 4th Density version of Earth, know that you will be choosing to lift the Veil that you co-created with the Annunaki, as part of the experience that you chose to have as a limited Human Being on a 3rd Density Earth. The technology, based on the Moon, that is used by those Beings to blind 3rd Density Humans to their multidimensional selves, will gradually lose its effectiveness upon you, as you move more deeply into 4th Density.

In practice, this means that you will experience, with increasing frequency, the simultaneous overlap of past lifetime, present lifetime, and future lifetime realities. Additionally, as stated elsewhere in this book, your telempathic abilities will grow, as will your ability to access other information and skills hitherto "hidden" from you, by you.

As a conscious creator/attractor of your life experiences, you will, frequently, be utilizing your imagination to create/attract something other than What-Is. In this sense, you will become more childlike. Life will become to you, as it is to children, an endless present moment in which to play. No worries; no rules; only fun.

If it is your desire to live in a UC, then, by paying attention to how you feel, and by always reaching for the best-feeling thought that you have access to in the moment, you will be unerringly guided by your Higher Self to the thoughts and actions that will create for/attract to you a wonderful life in a UC. By only, and always, reaching for and doing what feels good—by following your joy, your passion—you will always be in the right place at the right time to take the next step on your path to a happy life in a UC. And there will be no need to *pursue* the achievement of happiness at some distant, future point in time, as you will *be* happy in each and every now moment.

This is the transformational lifetime: *it's Now or Never.*

Printed in Great Britain
by Amazon